The United States Air Force Memorial Honor Guard

Honor Guard sculpture with Memorial Wall

The
United States
Air Force
Memorial
Honor Guard

A sculpture by
Zenos Frudakis

Main essay by
Rosalie Frudakis

Techni Press

ISBN 13: 978-0-615-16835-7
Library of Congress Control
Number: 2007907640

Techni Press
2355 Mount Carmel Avenue
Glenside, Pennsylvania
19038

RoFrudakis@aol.com

Designed by Nathan Garland
in New Haven, Connecticut.

Printed in Italy by Amilcare Pizzi.

Contents

The military Honor Guard has for centuries been the shining example of what is right and special about the military profession of arms: an ever present, ever vigilant, highly trained and professionally skilled group of warriors ready to defend our country when called to do so. And, so too in the Air Force — the youngest of America's military services — the Honor Guard represents the important military attributes of attention to detail, technical precision and professional competence that is second to none.

From my perspective, Zenos Frudakis, through his meticulous detailing of exacting uniform wear, hand and weapon position and ramrod bearing, highlights these special military attributes for all our Air Force Memorial visitors. Additionally, through the skillful crafting of strong faces with focused eyes, he captures the human element of the figures. The faces of the sculpture suggest depth of character and a very determined and unwavering mission purpose. Zenos' magnificent sculpture of an Honor Guard color team captures in a most visual way the very core of the United States Air Force, its people.

The importance of Zenos' sculpture to Airmen is readily apparent when one understands that an Honor Guard is ever present in the daily lives of our Air Force men and women. Whether honoring America by raising or lowering the US flag, performing ceremonial duties at important individual personal and professional career events — commissionings, enlistments, promotions or retirements — or folding the US flag over an Airman's coffin before burial, the Honor Guard is always there. The Honor Guard is vigilant, professional and respectful.

As the Managing Director of the Air Force Memorial Foundation, I have the opportunity to witness the effect that this larger than life sculpture has on our daily guests. Almost to a person, it achieves what we had hoped: a central "Kodak" moment to document one's visit to the Memorial. Whether it is the "little people" who slide in between or hug the legs of the figures or the "big people" who stand next to the figures and salute as their pictures are taken, most people want to remember the sculpture in a photo. The respect and appreciation visitors show these figures is a great testament to Zenos' artistic ability.

Mr. Zenos Frudakis' Honor Guard sculpture is a key, significant element of the United States Air Force Memorial. It provides a great mix of military tradition and human emotion, thus making it possible for all visitors — military or civilian — to make a personal connection, perhaps promoting a better understanding of what Airmen do for their country. The Honor Guard sculpture is ever present, ever on guard and ever vigilant as a symbolic guardian of our Air Force heritage, values and traditions. I salute and thank Zenos for capturing the spirit of America's Airmen with this sculpture.

Peter W. Lindquist
Colonel, USAF, Retired
Managing Director
Air Force Memorial Foundation
www.airforcememorial.org

Acknowledgements

Our profound appreciation to the following individuals, whose oversight of this project brought it from a concept to successful completion:

H. Ross Perot, Jr., Chairman, Board of Trustees, Air Force Memorial Foundation; Officers and Members of the Board of Trustees; General Robert Springer, USAF (Retired); Brigadier General Pat Adams, USAF (Retired); Major General Charles D. Link, USAF (Retired); Edward F. Grillo, Jr., Major General, USAF, (Retired) former President, Air Force Memorial Foundation; and especially Peter W. Lindquist, Colonel, USAF (Retired) Managing Director, Air Force Memorial Foundation. We wish to thank the Partners in the United States Air Force Memorial Project; the Board of Advisors; and the Project Teams.

We also thank the following for key guidance and support:
- Walter J. Boyne, Colonel, USAF (Retired)
- Architects James Ingo Freed and Kyle Johnson, Pei Cobb Freed & Partners

With special thanks to the following individuals for their part in the review process:
- Former CMSAF Gerald R. Murray
- Lieutenant Colonel Larry Hinkin formerly of HAF/CZ
- Representing the AFMF Honor Guard Review Committee at the final clay model review, Lieutenant General Robert Springer, USAF (Retired) and SMSergeant Joe Kuchera, USAF (Retired)

With gratitude and respect, we thank all the Honor Guard Specialists who advised on this sculpture including Elizabeth F. Adams, Major USAF, former Commander, USAF Honor Guard; Anthony Maisonet, Major USAF, former Commander USAF Honor Guard; Michael M. Buckley, Chief Master Sergeant USAF HG/CEM; Jamale R. Hart, Captain, USAF, former HG/HGD; Vincent T. Jackson, TSGT, USAF, former HG/HGCB; Jay Corales, Master Sergeant, USAF, former NCOIC, Colors Element, USAF HG; Lieutenant Colonel Gaylord Thomas, Former Commander USAF Honor Guard; Captain Nick Jameson, Former Operations Officer USAF Honor Guard; Honor Guardsmen of Bolling and Andrews Air Force Bases; Honor Guard alterations specialist Mrs. Chizuko Lowman; Master Sergeant Michael Bell; and Staff Sergeants Monique Townsend and San Juana Vasquez.

Our thanks and appreciation to the models for the sculptures, including Alexis Henry, Sergeant William Diaz and Airman First Class Nicol J. Sabol.

Special thanks to Laran Bronze Foundry, Chester, Pennsylvania owners Larry, Diane and Randy Welker, with our gratitude to them, Allen Ward and everyone on the foundry staff for their careful work, tireless efforts, excellence in their craft and consistent professionalism throughout this project.

Many thanks to Assisting Sculptors Jennifer Frudakis, Aaron J. Sykes and Christopher Collins.

For work on this publication: It has been our privilege to work with Nathan Garland, designer and editorial consultant; writers Dr. William Innes Homer and Katherine Jaeger; copy editors Kristina Klugar, Dianne Peich, Kathleen J. Stafford and Bruce E. Adams, Jr.; as well as Barbara Sadick and her colleagues at Arti Grafiche Amilcare Pizzi, s.p.a.

The success of this sculpture is due largely to collaboration with the above mentioned individuals affiliated with the United States Air Force.

RF and ZF

Dedicated to the men and women
who gave their lives while serving
in the United States Air Force

Guard of Honor

by Colonel Walter J. Boyne,
USAF, Retired, author of
*Soaring to Glory, The United States
Air Force Memorial*

The remarkable United States Air Force Memorial, with its soaring stainless steel spires, is a new phenomenon gracing the skyline of Washington, DC. Located on a promontory overlooking the Pentagon, and nestled near the sacred grounds of Arlington National Cemetery, the shape and size of the Memorial is a soaring tribute to the United States Air Force, one that was long overdue.

And of course, any tribute to the United States Air Force is in essence a tribute to the men and women who have made up that brilliant service and its predecessor organizations. While aircraft and missiles may capture the image of the Air Force in many instances, anyone who has served knows that no missile would be fired nor any aircraft be flown without the dedicated service of thousands of nameless men and women. This includes those who served in uniform or in civilian roles and also extends to the vital industries which make modern air power possible.

Thus it was essential that beneath the glittering silver spires of the Memorial, the very essence of the Air Force, its essential humanity, be captured in a form to which visitors could relate. And sculptor Zenos Frudakis did capture that essential humanity in his remarkable sculpture of the Honor Guard, which so faithfully depicts this colorful, emotionally evocative and always important element of the culture of the Air Force.

The 11th Wing at Bolling Air Force Base is the home of the United States Air Force Honor Guard, which Frudakis used as the model for his monumental sculpture.

The mission of the USAF Honor Guard is to maintain and employ a ceremonial capability to represent the United States Air Force at public and official ceremonies, including presidential inaugurations, the funerals of heads of state, and the arrival and departure ceremonies for visiting dignitaries. In doing so, the Honor Guard represents every man and woman in the Air Force, past present and future. The Honor Guard also participates in wreath-laying ceremonies at the Tomb of the Unknowns in Arlington, and at change of command and retirement ceremonies.

Bolling's famous Honor Guard is the model for similar Honor Guards that operate every day, all over the world at every important Air Force event, from changes of command or promotion ceremonies to funerals in local cemeteries. In every case, the members of each of these many local Honor Guards comport themselves with dignity and precision, lending credibility and importance to each event.

And in every case members of the Honor Guard are living breathing

human beings, filled with spirit. And it is this essential humanity which Frudakis so successfully portrays in his striking sculpture. Zenos is famous for his ability to portray individuals at the very height of their physical and mental capability and with his characteristic skill, he translated the living members of the USAF Honor Guard into the eight-foot, larger-than-life sculptures which form his work.

His sculpture, like all great works, went through many modifications before it achieved its final form. Originally, Zenos had planned a more representative, less exact sculpture, one that would accommodate probable changes in uniform over the decades. In time, as he became more familiar with the members of the Air Force Memorial Foundation, and with the members of the Honor Guard, Zenos allowed himself to execute the sculpture in a very precise way, detailing every element of each uniform with uncanny precision. Yet at the same time, he managed to have his work capture the essential humanity of his models. Frudakis refused to have his sculptured figures become static; instead, he wanted them to reflect the full range of emotions that his models possessed in such great abundance. And in this he succeeded brilliantly. His Honor Guard seems ready to march forth, its bronze flags flying, at a simple word of command.

Now his sculpture stands proudly on the grounds of the United States Air Force Memorial, and has become the ideal spot for photo opportunities for visitors. More importantly, the Honor Guard created by Zenos Frudakis for the Air Force Memorial fulfills the same role as a living Honor Guard might, maintaining a constant salute, night and day, to all the members of the United States Air Force and its predecessor organizations.

Facing page:
Honor Guard sculpture,
rear view

The Air Force Memorial

This last United States military branch memorial to be created in commemoration of the four branches of the United States' Armed Forces overlooks the Pentagon, the Potomac River and the nation's capital. The Air Force Memorial Honor Guard sculpture is to the Air Force what the Iwo Jima sculpture is to the Marines.

At the highest point in Arlington National Cemetery, a tract of land formerly known as the Naval Annex contains three spires — the tallest rising 270 feet in the air — that marks the location of this Memorial. These spires, designed to resemble the "bomb burst" maneuver performed by the USAF Thunderbird Demonstration Team, are highly visible from a distance, leading visitors to the Memorial grounds. There, the Honor Guard sculpture, standing at attention, greets the Memorial's visitors with its solemn presence. This sculpture gives a human face to the Memorial — a powerful reminder of its purpose — remembrance of sacrifice and solace for those who remain behind.

The United States Air Force Memorial Honor Guard

The United States Air Force (USAF) Honor Guard provides military funeral honors for active duty, retired members, and veterans of the USAF, and performs symbolic activities at special duty ceremonies including —

- Armed Forces full honor arrival ceremonies at the White House for the President and foreign heads of state, Joint Service and Air Force ceremonies;

- State funerals, Air Force funerals held at Arlington National Cemetery and Air Force funerals in proximity to the national capital region; and

- USAF Honor Guard precision rifle drill team exhibitions.

All Honor Guard activities emphasize the importance of military customs and courtesies, dress and appearance, and drill and ceremonies.

Facing page:
Memorial spires with
Honor Guard sculpture

Figurative Military
Memorial Sculpture:
An Overview

by Katherine Jaeger

Across the United States in almost every city park, town square, or public cemetery, stone soldiers stand sentry at their cannons, bronze generals wield their swords astride charging horses, and granite admirals point their spyglasses at distant horizons. Civil War battlefields bristle with sculptural markers of all kinds, and military tombs sport stone carvings and bronze reliefs as well as sculptures in the round. Historians are only now beginning to catalog and chronicle these treasures, city by city and state by state. They are discovering that many of America's military memorials are works of great artistic distinction.

For its first 75 years, the new nation was preoccupied with its survival. The enormous expense of setting up a government, building a capital, and acquiring and developing new territory meant that few national resources could be devoted to looking backward or memorializing. While Congress did award exquisite medals to military leaders of the Revolution, the War of 1812, and the War with Mexico, all other commemoration of military effort remained the province of local authorities. Until the 1850s, the paucity of trained sculptors and absence of bronze foundries prevented the creation of monuments.

A pair of sculptors who happened to be good friends changed all that. Clark Mills, who in 1848 accepted a White House commission for a monumental statue of General Andrew Jackson for Lafayette Square in Washington, built the country's first sculptural foundry in Maryland to cast the work. After years of trial and error with the process, he unveiled his portrait of Jackson on a rearing mount to great acclaim in 1853. The New York Times reported:

> The Washington people are in ecstasies with their equestrian statue. The first appearance of this piece of art calls forth unbounded enthusiasm....It was certainly a great day for Mr. Mills, and if his work encourages in our countrymen a taste for sculptural adornments in our public gardens and squares, then it will prove to have been a good day for us all.

Sculptor Henry Kirke Brown, who followed his friend's casting tribulations with great interest, had erected his own foundry in Brooklyn, New York, in 1848. Here he successfully produced smaller pieces such as busts of statesmen, but for his first military statue for Manhattan's Union Square, he used the services of Ames Manufacturing Company, a heavy-duty weapons founder of Massachusetts. His monumental equestrian George Washington, unveiled in 1856, received nationwide publicity and unanimous applause. On Washington's birthday, 1858, Thomas Crawford's imposing version of an equestrian Washington was unveiled in Richmond, Virginia, attracting even more attention. Commentators proclaimed that indeed, America's heroes were as important as the heroes of Europe, and deserved to be enshrined for posterity by her most accomplished artists, as had been done in Europe for centuries.

The Robert Gould Shaw Memorial,
bronze, Augustus Saint-Gaudens,
unveiled in 1897, Boston,
Massachusetts, the Common

These events might have sparked a wave of new monument construction had not the Civil War (1861-1865) intervened. The government became preoccupied with the needs of war and had no resources to spare for commemorative art. When it was over, the all-consuming processes of reunification and reconstruction began. It was not until the early 1870s that national finances and public spirits had recovered enough for Americans to consider erecting monuments. They perceived that sculptors, with their works of timeless and durable beauty, could help heal the wounds of war. Monuments would not only honor those who fought and fell; they would preserve their deeds in memory for future generations.

The national centennial of 1876 had its impact as well. In the course of preparing for that anniversary, many citizens began to think of the United States as having a history worth celebrating. They wanted to enshrine the acts of not only the participants in the Civil War, but of all American wars. In 1873, the city of Concord, New Hampshire, commissioned native son Daniel Chester French to create a statue to the revolutionary Minutemen. In 1874, a committee of New Yorkers hired John Quincy Adams Ward to create a monument to its 7th Regiment of Civil War volunteers. Soon across the country, public and private committees were raising funds for indoor statues and busts and outdoor monuments of all kinds. As more foundries were built and more artists traveled to Europe for training in sculptural modeling and carving, the quality of their output improved. Today's sculpture historians refer to the period 1875-1917 as the "American Renaissance," partly because of its innovations and advances, and partly due to its wide public support for the art form.

More than any other 19th century work, the monument to Civil War General Robert G. Shaw and his 54th Massachusetts Regiment of black volunteers attracted America's interest in public memorial art. When it was unveiled in Boston in 1897, it awakened governmental and civic leaders to what could be achieved when a great artist approached a military subject.

Back in 1865, Governor S.G. Howe and members of his senate had conceived the idea of an equestrian portrait of Shaw, who at tremendous personal risk had led black citizens of the North against Southern forces fighting to sustain the practice of slavery. Shaw had been slain at the battle of Fort Wagner near Charleston, South Carolina in 1863, and residents of Massachusetts clamored for a permanent testimonial to his sacrifice. By 1866, a memorial committee had collected $3,200 through private donations and public subscription. It grew through investment to $16,500, enough to hire an eminent sculptor to undertake the work.

Portrait studies for Shaw Memorial,
plaster, Augustus Saint-Gaudens,
Saint-Gaudens National Historic Site,
Cornish, New Hampshire

Augustus Saint-Gaudens had gained wide recognition for his memorial to Admiral David G. Farragut for New York's Madison Square, erected in 1881. During his 12-year labor on the Shaw, he was in such demand that he received several additional major commissions, including a monument to General William Tecumseh Sherman for New York's Central Park. When the Shaw was finally unveiled on Boston Common opposite the State House in early 1897, Saint-Gaudens admitted that he had spent more time thinking about it and altering its design, than working on it. Though the delay was frustrating to the committee that had planned for completion in two years, the public considered it entirely worthwhile. Saint-Gaudens, with architect-collaborators Charles McKim and Stanford White, was the first American sculptor to consider the importance of the landscape setting, the visitor's point of view, and the architecture of the support and surround. He believed that all these things must work together to create a unified monumental vision. He was the first to depict a whole column of soldiers, thereby honoring not just the General but the rank and file. His uncompromising attention to detail produced a masterpiece. In 1897 commentator William Coffin wrote —

> See what variety of type and gradations of expression are shown in these heads, and note the rhythm of the march, the individuality of the bodies, of the arms and legs and hands and feet. Every part of the relief bears testimony to the skill of the sculptor and to his analytical powers. But stand back and look at the work as a whole. How unified and complete it is! With what force is the general effect brought to one, making him feel the grandeur of the whole!

What was new here was the feeling. Where previous monuments had provoked admiration for their great size or artistic realism, or wonderment at the technical processes of their creation, Saint-Gaudens' work produced strong emotion. The soldiers' faces and attitudes suggested the grave risk they took; and in the forward momentum of their figures, viewers could feel the resolve and effort of their march to war. The composition radiated determined energy, imparting a powerful experience to the visitor.

Creators of 20th century memorials incorporated Saint-Gaudens' lessons in myriad ways. More monument designers gave attention to siting, landscaping, and illumination, and carefully evaluated the impact of particular construction materials and unity of presentation between sculptural and architectural elements. As cities filled up with public sculpture and memorial committees competed for dwindling unoccupied space, the idea of making each monument an "experience" took hold. The government garnered a more prominent role in dictating what subject matter could be memorialized, and procedures for gaining approval became more involved. Today, in Washington, DC, the

Commission of Fine Arts, the National Capital Planning Commission, the American Battle Monuments Commission, and the National Capital Memorial Commission all have oversight of the many decisions that go into making a military memorial.

Though the Abraham Lincoln Monument Association formed two years after the Civil War Commander-in-Chief was assassinated in 1867, the group did not manage to approve a site for the memorial until 1901. Construction began on the magnificent Doric temple by architect Henry Bacon in 1914. With the death of Saint-Gaudens in 1907, French had assumed the position of America's most respected sculptor, so it was only natural that he be chosen to create the awe-inspiring 19-foot-high seated statue of Lincoln that would form the centerpiece of Bacon's interior. The success of this marvelous work, executed in white Georgian marble and installed in 1923, assured French's lasting influence on future generations of sculptors.

No memorials are more emotionally powerful or beloved than the national war memorials authorized by Congress. The US Marine Corps War Memorial, unveiled in November 1954, was a successful 20th-century member of this group. Its conceptual committee was charged with choosing one scene or image from the entire history of the Marine Corps that would have meaning for every member — from the aged Spanish American War veteran to the recently retired World War II leatherneck, to all the recruits of future centuries. The choice was clear; it must be Joe Rosenthal's celebrated February 23, 1945 photograph, "Old Glory Goes up on Mount Suribachi, Iwo Jima," taken during one of the fiercest Pacific theater battles of World War II. From the moment the Associated Press distributed this shot less than 24 hours after it was taken, it became an international icon of US military effort, and a matter of special pride to the Marines.

In 1945, sculptor Felix de Weldon had created a nine-foot plaster model of the flag-raising scene which toured the country as part of the war bond effort. Public response to his work was so warm that Congress awarded him the sculpture commission, and named architect Horace W. Peaslee as its site designer. Peaslee made one modification that would heighten the impact of the now-familiar scene; he enlarged it to gigantic proportions. The 32-foot tall figures standing atop a 10-foot high granite base with the flagpole lofting another 16 feet above the group was to be one of the world's largest bronze statues. Its site, an eight-acre promontory on Arlington Ridge, included a military parade ground and afforded plenty of room for viewers to contemplate it from different angles.

Subsequent military memorial projects in Washington continued to employ sculpted figures. Three bronze soldiers created by Frederick

The United States Marine Corps War Memorial, also known as the Iwo Jima Memorial, based on the Associated Press photo by Joe Rosenthal, Arlington National Cemetery, 1954, Arlington, Virginia

Hart complemented the Vietnam Veterans Memorial Wall (1992), while the Korean War Veterans Memorial (1995) included 19 figures of stainless steel. The World War II Memorial (2004) employed 24 bas-relief panels to incorporate the human element. In 2006, the Air Force Memorial both upholds tradition and extends it in a new direction. Zenos Frudakis' Honor Guard group is an integral part of the Memorial design; it returns the visitor's gaze to earth, balancing the dramatic skyward thrust of the stainless steel spires. As Professor Homer outlines in his essay, the sculptor's technique manifests the wealth of knowledge gained from forbearers like Augustus Saint-Gaudens and Daniel Chester French. As Rosalie Frudakis recounts, Frudakis' rendering, like the memorials of Shaw and Lincoln, entailed a tremendous amount of research, review, and revision.

The emotional chord struck by Frudakis' Honor Guard, however, is unlike Shaw's determined volunteers marching to war, jubilant Marines scrambling to declare victory, or any other war memorial. Instead, it imparts the serene and solemn dignity of a military funeral. Anyone who has witnessed an Honor Guard in attendance at a burial can instantly identify the contemplative mixture of respect, sorrow, and pride seen in Frudakis' figures.

Honor Guard sculpture,
detail of all four figures

On Acknowledging
the Human Presence
in Art

by Rosalie Frudakis

A museum director with whom I once worked told me the following story. Early in her career, while teaching art history at a college in Maine, she took her students on a class trip to the Museum of Fine Arts in Boston. Some of the students were parents, so she encouraged those students to bring their children along.

The group moved through the Museum of Fine Arts with her guidance, at one point assembling in an exhibition hall presenting Egyptian art. She noticed one of the children, a little girl about five years old, crossing the gallery to join her mother who was with the group. The child passed in front of two large statues of an Egyptian king and queen. She glanced over at the sculptures and stopped. She turned and faced them for a moment, unsure of herself. She then looked directly at them, curtseyed to the sculptures, and continued on her way.

This little girl, too young to have attended public school, too young to have learned about the Egyptians or the significance of these particular works of art, nevertheless felt something while she was in their presence. She knew these were representations of people, important people, and they needed to be addressed respectfully and acknowledged as such.

I recall the museum director's story because I think it speaks to the power of art, especially the power of the human form in art. When we view any figurative art, we relate to the forms as human beings, from the most ancient art — like the energetic cave paintings of horses and other animals in Southern France — to the most current figurative works. Circling Rodin's *Burghers of Calais* and "walking among them" as Rodin asked of us, we feel the pathos of these men. If we do not know the history of this work, we begin to ask questions. What were these men doing? Why are they posed as they are?

Through answers to these questions, which lead in turn to more questions, we begin to understand something more about the human condition. Like the little girl in the museum, we do not have to be highly educated to recognize that the human figure speaks to us because it is eternal, as ancient as the human race and as modern as each person living today.

Figurative art has this power to relate to and connect with the viewer. In the case of the Honor Guard, these figures convey a solemn and palliative presence, respectful of those whose lives have been sacrificed while offering solace for those who remain.

I am Rosalie Frudakis, Zenos' partner of 32 years in the sculpture studio, and I am honored to share the journey we took as we created the United States Air Force Memorial Honor Guard sculpture.

Facing page:
Early clay sketch
of Honor Guard
as bas-relief

Creating the
Honor Guard
Sculpture

by Rosalie Frudakis

The Board of Directors of the Air Force Memorial Foundation (AFMF) decided to include a sculpture of the Honor Guard as part of the United States Air Force Memorial for Arlington National Cemetery, Virginia. The sculpture itself — 16 feet in height — consists of four eight-foot bronze figures, patinaed in blue-gray, standing side by side, mounted on a 10- by two-foot long bronze base. Two of the figures are flag bearers, one holding an eight-foot tall United States flag and the other an Air Force flag, complete with battle streamers, each weighing 700 pounds; the other two figures, flanking the flag bearers, are rifle guards weighing 450 pounds each. The sculpture is positioned in front of one of two inscription walls located within the Memorial's landscaped park; the 12-inch thick walls each measure 10 feet high by 56 feet.

Asked to find a sculptor, Pete Lindquist spoke with Frederick Hart, sculptor of the soldiers at the National Vietnam Memorial, who referred Zenos to the AFMF. Upon review of Zenos' portfolio, the AFMF asked him to sculpt the Honor Guard.

Becoming
Informed

In preparation for any new work, Zenos collects and reviews all available documentation on his new subject. Research for this project included a careful study of photos and film of the Air Force Honor Guard as well as personal interviews. He took hundreds of photos of the current Honor Guard from all possible views. He took close-ups of their uniforms — their shoes, pants and sleeves, and their positions while in motion and at rest. He took shots to see how bearing the weight of flags, battle streamers and ceremonial weapons affected their stance, balance and motion as well as the creases in their uniforms. In the case of the female Honor Guard, he recorded her hairstyle.

Several visits to Andrews and Bolling Air Force Bases were made possible by the AFMF for the purpose of interviewing members of the Honor Guard and photographing them in action.

Zenos and I were overwhelmed by the amount of explicit detail present in every aspect of Honor Guard culture. We were also impressed with the commitment of these young men and women to the Honor Guard, their devotion to their work, and their skill at presentation and exacting movements. They patiently explained anything we wanted to know and showed us the many nuances of Honor Guard dress and practices. They showed us, for example, how one must judge the distance between one's face and the flagpole — by counting finger widths from the nose — and how some guardsmen tape down their ties to guard against the vagaries of the wind. Some keep important directions and other information inside their hats.

The Honor Guard, Bolling Air
Force Base, 11th Wing

Initial design plans for the Honor Guard sculpture called for granite, not bronze. It took the form of a low relief on the surface of a thick stone wall. Zenos thought this heavy, earth-bound idea was antithetical to the Air Force and what it represents: an airborne combat force. He advised the AFMF that the subject of the Honor Guard would be better presented — and less expensive — if it were translated into bronze, explaining that bronze could be a much more exciting material for this sculpture. The play of light on bronze would convey the sense of motion in the figures even in stillness, the light flickering on the metal evoking a level of excitement intrinsic to the material. In addition, the metal, although not the same as that used in airplanes, would be more akin to aircraft than stone. To move the sculpture from stone to bronze was to shift it toward the realistic and away from the decorative concept of shallow surface carving on a massive piece of stone.

A further complication of the original concept occurred as the back of the stone relief repeated the wall behind it. Visitors could stand between these two walls, leaving the question of what to do with an otherwise blank wall confronting the public.

Zenos suggested that he create several sculptures for the AFMF showing the Honor Guard in three levels of relief — low, mezzo and high. While all relief sculpture presents figures against a solid background, low relief is sculpture lightly etched against this background, mezzo relief is a more boldly articulated sculpture, and high relief is the most generously formed sculpture against a supporting wall.

Releasing the sculptures from their wall entirely, Zenos also created one set of figures in the round — one set of figures stood on its own without any background whatsoever. He intended to show the AFMF that the sculptures looked better as they moved out of the wall and were best seen without any supporting wall. When the Board of AFMF subsequently chose the sculpture in the round to be developed further, the move from stone to bronze inevitably followed. Once the sculpture moved from bas-relief to sculpture in the round, granite would be impractical for carving the weapons, flags, and delicate battle streamers.

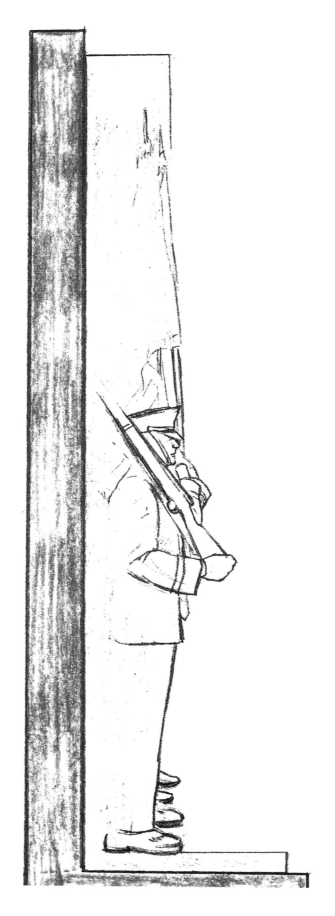

Early drawing
for clay sketch
of Honor Guard
as bas-relief

Before the 24-inch high figures were further developed, Zenos created a nine-inch high model in clay. The positioning of all figures was worked out in this size, as it was easier to make changes in this version than in subsequent larger sculptures. This small, rough model is called a maquette, the French word derived from the Italian macchietta, meaning sketch.

The Board approved the maquette, permitting Zenos to develop the 24-inch high Honor Guard figures in the round. While the 24-inch model was in progress, the Board discussed the final size of the work. While the AFMF wanted the Honor Guard sculpture to measure six feet in height, or life-size, Zenos pointed out that space and light appear to shrink sculpture placed outdoors, significantly diminishing the impact of the pieces in the large Memorial. He suggested that the sculpture be larger than life size, and the Board approved the creation of a nine-foot high model in clay. Zenos believed that increased height would work well in the space, adding dignity and decorum.

A Change of Venue   Originally the Memorial was to be located on Arlington Ridge. The Marines considered the newest Memorial to be too close to the Iwo Jima sculpture. The AFMF found a new site for its Memorial at the former Navy Annex. The highest land in the area, it seemed a more appropriate site for the Memorial.

A New Challenge   After the Board of Directors of the AFMF and architects James Ingo Freed and Kyle Johnson viewed Zenos' nine-foot high clay models in progress at Laran Bronze Foundry in Chester, PA, the US Commission of Fine Arts (USCFA) indicated it would insist the sculpture be eight feet high with no base, flush with the ground. This commentary was unusual, as nearly all sculptures have a bronze base that rests on a stone to assure their balance.

With the approval of the Board, Zenos started over, sculpting an Honor Guard sculpture eight feet high. Having already created several small, intermediate and large models, the eight-foot high model developed quickly.

In studio, *Honor Guard sculpture*
eight-feet high in clay, 24-inch
high intermediate model in plaster
and nine-inch high clay macquette
with flags in foreground

Flags and Battle Streamers While Zenos worked on the eight-foot high version of the Honor Guard sculpture, the Board held discussions about the flags and battle streamers. Were real flags and battle streamers to be used with this sculpture, or were they to be sculpted? Zenos advocated for the flags and battle streamers to be sculpted in clay and cast in bronze; his thinking was that to do otherwise might make the Honor Guard figures appear to be elaborate flag-holders. He reasoned: Why stop at the flags? If the flags were to be real, why not the ceremonial weapons? Or the belts or hats?

The AFMF invited Zenos to meet with the USCFA. Composed of seven members appointed by the President, the USCFA was established in 1910 to advise the government on architectural development in the District of Columbia. It is authorized to give recommendations on the location of statues, fountains and monuments in public spaces. Past members included landscape architect Frederick Law Olmstead, Jr., and artists Daniel Chester French, Paul Manship and Frederick Hart.

The USCFA agreed that the flags and battle streamers should be bronze, and the Board of the AFMC authorized Zenos to sculpt them in clay. The puzzle of how to sculpt them accurately included the process of learning about the battle streamers, what they are, what they represent, their importance to the Honor Guard, and their significance.

The Air Force Ceremonial Departmental Flag is displayed with a set of campaign streamers, each one recognizing a particular battle or campaign fought by the Air Force, beginning with the Mexican Expedition (1916-17). Campaign credits prior to 1947, when the Air Force was part of the Army, are also commemorated by streamers on the Army Ceremonial Flag. Each streamer carries the name of the battle and its date. The streamers are assembled on the pole with the earliest battle first. Each subsequent battle streamer is added so the most recent battles appear toward the top of the group.

In studio, battle
streamers in clay

39

Zenos' original proposal to the AFMF requested that the sculpture be sketchy, with a loosely handled surface, treating the figures in a more painterly manner.

Referencing sculpture by Daniel Chester French, who created the Lincoln Memorial, and Augustus Saint-Gaudens, sculptor of the Adams and Shaw Memorials, Zenos remarked that details present in many successful sculptures yielded to the forms and actions of the figures; details were not a focus. He noted that fashion changes, and in several decades, the Honor Guard uniform would also change in appearance, perhaps making the sculpture appear dated.

The AFMF Board approved this sketch-like approach to the sculpture. As members of the 11th Wing, Bolling Air Force Base's United States Air Force Honor Guard began their studio visits, the approach to the treatment of the sculpture changed radically. Reviewing the sculptures as they would fellow Guardsmen, they politely noted lists of changes amounting to between one and four pages of revisions to the sculpture per visit. These lists were confirmed in writing between the studio and the AFMF, and the changes were made. These included slight changes in the position of the feet, the relationship of the figures to each other, the positioning of the hands on the ceremonial weapons and in relationship to the bodies of the figures, the positioning of the heads, necks, arms and legs of the figures, their eyes and ears, and an entire cornucopia of details we thought were perfect, but that we had missed by a hair. After each visit, several e-mail exchanges invariably took place to double-check or confirm aspects of the Honor Guard.

Subsequent visits focused more and more on details, moving the sculpture to the complete opposite of its original sketch-like design. Measurements were taken by eye, by finger-widths, by referral to photographs of the Honor Guard lining the studio walls, and by rulers, with accuracy reaching the smallest fractions of an inch. The Honor Guardsmen shared every device they employed to ensure precise measurements for positioning clothing, ties, medals, buttons, shoes, straps, belts, accessories, flags, and ceremonial weapons.

Some of the notes taken and changes made included moving the spade-shape on top of the flag-pole so it was visible from the front view; making one single break in the pants as they hit the shoe; measuring one-half inch from the bottom of the pocket and placing the medals there; placing the USAF Honor Guards' round "cookie" badge one-half inch beneath these medals; making sure the chin strap was right on the edge of the chin and the buckle on each facing to the right; removing dimples in the ties and moving them as high as possible; and spacing the belt one thumb-width on each side of the belt loops and centering it between the two buttons on the jacket.

Facing page:
Mrs. Chizuko Lowman,
Honor Guard
alterations specialist,
demonstrates
her "finger-width"
measurement

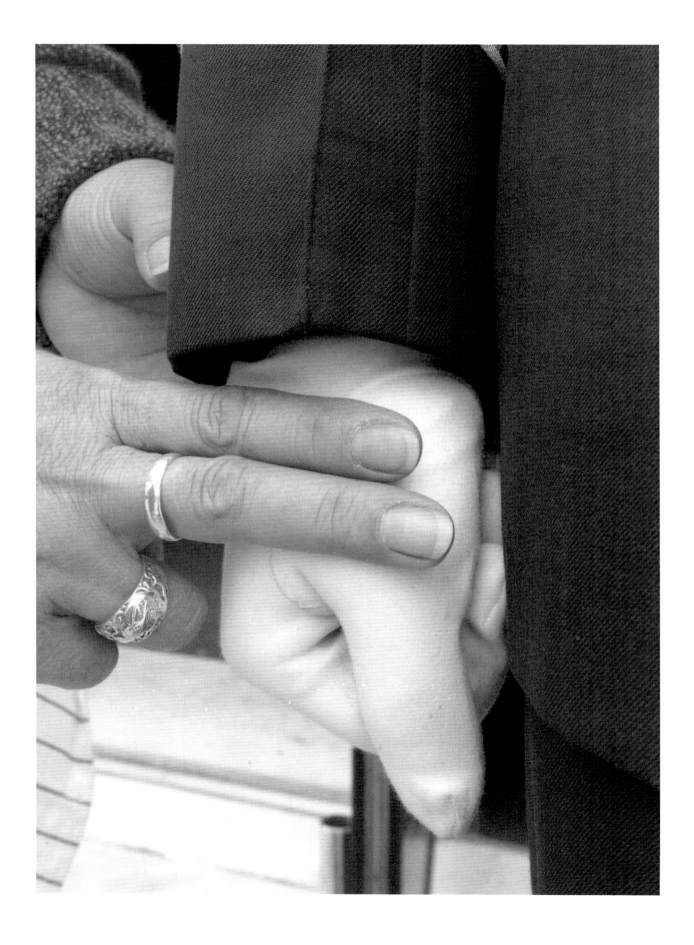

After many visits and reviews, Zenos asked the Honor Guardsmen to remember that he was a sculptor and not a tailor. As the result of this collaboration of sculptor and Honor Guardsmen, the sculpture grew more and more precise in every aspect.

As the sculpture developed, the AFMF loaned the studio flags and a set of battle streamers to Zenos to study and review throughout the process of creating these objects in clay.

The sculptures became so detailed that upon what was hoped to be the final review and approval of the sculpture, the shoelaces of the sculptures were found to be crossed incorrectly. The shoelaces had to be re-sculpted to show the lead shoelace crossing from the Guardsman's left to his/her right, and the sculptures required an additional review before final Board approval was granted.

Throughout the process of creating the Honor Guard sculpture, Zenos produced other commissioned work. One of these works contained some similarities to the Honor Guard sculpture, and many more differences. Freedom, a series of four over-life size, sketchy figures in various stages of escaping from a bronze wall, was commissioned by Liberty Property Trust for GlaxoSmithKline World Headquarters in Philadelphia. At one point, with the two sculptures standing on opposite sides of the studio, it was not difficult to compare and contrast the Freedom and the Honor Guard sculpture — the first in various degrees of motion, the second completely static. Zenos was committed to making the standing figures of the Honor Guard sculpture as full of life as possible for stationary figures.

In order to have non-tiring, non-moving models consistently available to wear uniforms, male and female mannequins acquired by the studio were dressed in Honor Guard uniforms borrowed from the AFMF. These uniforms were adjusted during each studio visit by Honor Guard specialists, who restored belts, medals, buttons and accessories to their accurate positions.

Facing page:
Elizabeth F. Adams, Major USAF, former Commander, USAF Honor Guard, reviews position of cap on Honor Guardsman at Bolling Air Force Base

Studio Models   While acknowledging that the vital role of the Honor Guard's
precision and formality is integral to the ceremonies in which they
engage, Zenos felt strongly that the sculpture needed to convey
the breathing presences of the real men and women who comprise
this special unit. The challenge was to infuse life into figures that
were, by necessity, stationary.

Initial plans for the Honor Guard sculpture called for generic
uniformed figures without race or gender. As the originally proposed
"sketchy" figures became more and more specific under the guidance
of the Honor Guard specialists, it was natural that the portraits on
the sculptures needed to project more personality. The US Fine Arts
Commission ordered Zenos to make specific portraits on the figures,
and the Board of Directors for the AFMF authorized that order.

Recalling the women and the Hispanic and African-American men
who participated in the Honor Guard ceremonies at Bolling, Zenos
requested the Board's permission to make the Honor Guard sculpture
reflect the diversity inherent in the US military and the Honor
Guard units he observed. The Board approved this recommendation
immediately.

Facing page:
Staff Sergeant Anthony Frazier,
Honor Guardsman, Bolling
Air Force Base, 11th Wing,
demonstrating position of cap,
chin strap, medals, and flag

The Honor Guard sculpture for the Air Force Memorial is composed, from left to right, of one Caucasian man, one African-American man, one Hispanic man and one Caucasian woman. The sculptures of both the Caucasian man and the African-American man were created with the help of several models posing for each figure. The sculpture of the Hispanic Airman was drawn from Sergeant William Diaz, of the US Air Force Reserves 913th Services in Willow Grove, Pennsylvania, several miles from Zenos' Glenside studio. Sergeant Diaz said of his studio experience, "It was truly an honor to pose for something I believe in. I am proud of what and whom it represents. To play a part in this history is beyond words, and working with Zenos was an experience I will never forget. He taught me the value of looking at life through the eyes of an artist."

Facing page:
Sergeant William Diaz
poses in studio

Alexis Henry posed in uniform for the female Guardsman; her portrait graces the sculpture. Airman First Class Nicol J. Sabol, at that time, with the 913 Air Force Communications Flight in Willow Grove, also posed. She said, "I was interested in modeling for the sculpture and being part of the Memorial. It isn't often that you get a chance to be part of history."

Facing page:
In studio, Zenos with clay bust of female Honor Guardsman, portrait based on Alexis Henry

Following four pages:
Sergeant William Diaz poses for bust

Zenos Frudakis (left) and assisting sculptor Aaron Sykes (right) with clay models in the studio

Assisting Sculptors   Zenos' niece, Jennifer Frudakis, a professional sculptor with her own career of several decades, assisted throughout the development of the large figures. In 2004 and 2005, Aaron J. Sykes, who assisted on World War II Memorial sculptures, worked on the clay models with Zenos and Jennifer. In 2005 and 2006, sculptor and painter Christopher Collins assisted with the flags and battle streamers.

Facing page:
Assisting sculptors
Christopher Collins and
Jennifer Frudakis
working on clay flags

The Casting Process

For the last 22 years, Zenos has cast all his bronzes at Laran Bronze Foundry (www.laranbronze.com). Owned by Lawrence Welker III, his wife Diane and his brother Randy, Laran Bronze is a full-service sculpture foundry located in the former Sun Ship Building in Chester, Pennsylvania. The Honor Guard sculpture was transformed into bronze in this building, which was formerly devoted to manufacturing oil tankers for World War II and constructing ships.

After a final visit for review of the sculptures by AFMF President Major General Edward F. Grillo, Jr., USAF Retired and Vice President of Operations Colonel Peter W. Lindquist, USAF Retired, and upon approval of the eight-foot high clay models by the Board, Laran Bronze began the long process of casting the sculpture in bronze using the lost wax process.

Facing page:
Mold, upper torso,
at Laran Bronze Foundry

Following four pages:
Wax casts

Clay legs in background,
rubber molds and plaster
mother molds

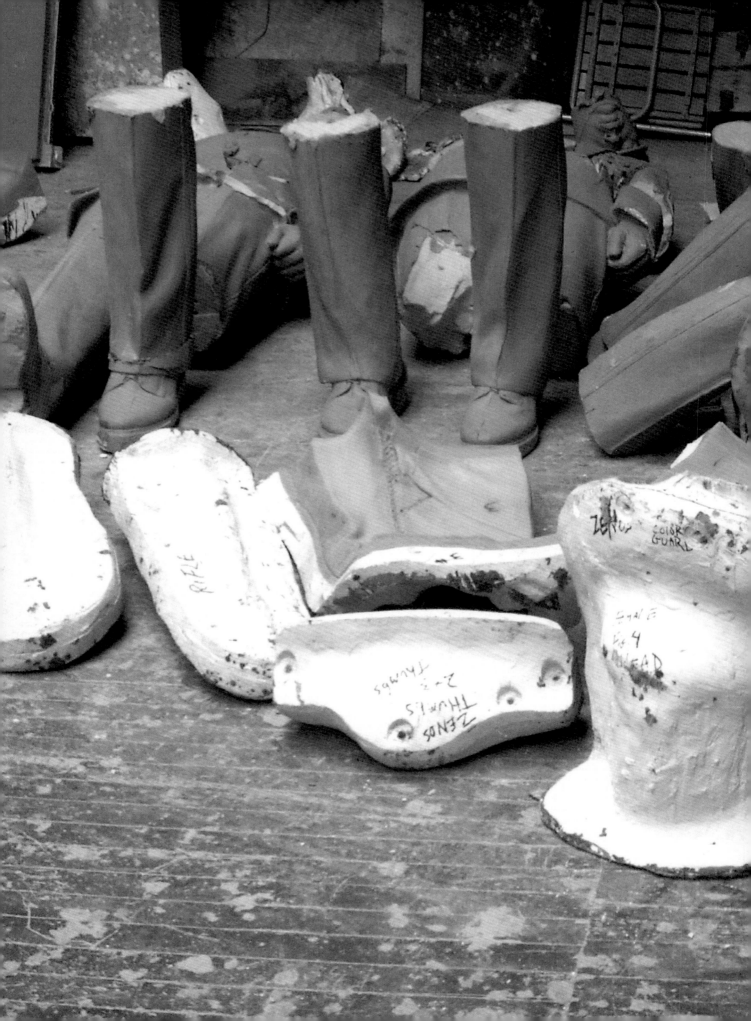

The ceramic shell was then taken out of the kiln, and molten bronze, heated to 2,100 degrees Fahrenheit, was poured into it. After cooling for several hours, the shell was broken away with hammers to reveal the bronze cast. Fragments of ceramic shell were sand-blasted away and the sculpture was reviewed. All the individual parts of the sculpture cast into bronze were welded together. Indications of welding, including seams and spots, were ground away with metal tools. Zenos "chased" (hand-carved) the bronze to restore details.

Upon completion of this process, the sculptures were reviewed by General Grillo, Pete Lindquist and several Honor Guard specialists before the patina (surface coloring) was applied.

Laran Bronze President Larry Welker commented about casting the Honor Guard sculpture: "The most difficult part was casting the flags, because of the folds. Everything had to line up perfectly, and this was challenging." During the assembly process, Major General Grillo viewed the sculptures and assisted the foundry men in correctly aligning the folds on the flags.

Larry recalled, "After the sculpture was completely assembled and Randy and I assessed the work as plumb and true, the architect's slope dimensions presented concerns. According to the architect's plan, the bronze base of the sculpture was required to be flush with the granite flooring of the Memorial. We had to take that pitch into consideration and construct a jig that would accommodate the slope. This also meant we had to correct for the armature by changing the left foot of each figure." Altering an already-cast sculpture is no easy feat. The necessary adjustments required many additional hours of labor.

A great deal of consideration was given to the choice of patina. Zenos felt the traditional brown patina would not complement the stainless steel and stone in the surrounding area. As blue is the color of the Air Force uniforms, he thought a blue-gray patina would resonate better with these materials. Zenos wanted to distinguish the Air Force Memorial Honor Guard sculpture by this color to keep it from being dismissed as just another constellation of brown bronze figures. He shared his ideas with architect James Ingo Freed who first leaned toward the traditional brown bronze, but reconsidered and changed his opinion in time. The AFMF felt the blue-gray patina was a good choice, and so did the US Commission of Fine Arts. The Board approved the patina and the process of surface coloring was started.

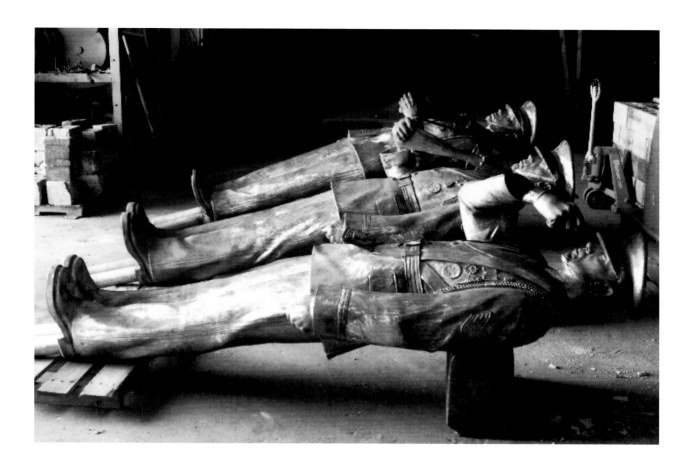

The bronzes were heated with blow-torches, and chemicals were applied with brushes to achieve surface coloring. In order to make the blue surface color stand, chemicals that comprise this patina were separated from the bronze itself by a first patina of black on the bronze. After the black patina was created, chemicals that form the blue patina were applied. A sealing wax which also contained elements that support the blue-gray patina was applied to the surface of the bronze to seal it.

Facing page:
Bronze figures with flags and battle streamers completed

Following four pages:
Wrapping one figure at the foundry

Moving the figures to the site

Engineered to withstand hurricane force winds, the Honor Guard sculpture is secure at the site of the Air Force Memorial. Installing the work at the site, however, presented a number of logistical challenges for Laran Bronze Foundry. First, the metal base of the sculpture was installed and made level with the granite. This process required the tedious and exacting raising and lowering of the base to align the protruding stainless steel rods with corresponding nuts until the base was level with the stone. Grout pumped underneath the base had to cure for 24 hours, so the foundry men expected to return the following day to install the sculptures.

The installation crew assembled at the foundry the day after Labor Day, 2006, at 4:30 am to deliver the sculpture to the Arlington site.

Because cranes were not available due to heavy rain, the sculptures, each figure strapped to a skid, were delivered below the site of the memorial using a front loader while rain continued to pour. In better weather the following day, Larry said, "To install the sculptures, we worked with a crane operator on the site, but the crane was located behind the wall. My brother Randy was positioned on the wall in order to signal the crane operator, who then raised the sculptures one at a time up the 40-foot high hill, over the wall and across the Memorial grounds to where I was at installation site." Larry and the installation crew then carefully guided the sculptures into position, where they proudly stand today.

Facing page:
Positioning one figure
at the site

The ceremony was held in Arlington, Virginia, on Saturday, October 14, 2006. It began the service's 60th Anniversary Commemoration, From Heritage to Horizons — Commemorating 60 Years of Air and Space Power. The day was beautiful. The weather cooperated as if following orders, an irony not lost on some. Spirits were high.

The public was invited to visit the Air Force Open House beginning at 9:00 am in the Pentagon South Parking Area. Interactive and static displays of equipment, helicopters and aircraft included the Predator and Global Hawk unmanned aerial vehicles; UH-1, HH-60, MH-53 helicopters; the CV-22 tilt-rotor aircraft; and an F-35 Joint Strike Fighter display model. The Air Force Honor Guard Drill Team and the Air Force Band performed and a live simulcast of the dedication was visible in this location.

At 1:30 pm at the Memorial site, the formal dedication ceremony began. Massive viewing screens were set up so the audience could better see the ceremony.

Facing page:
Honor Guard sculpture
with spires

Program books included letters from President George W. Bush, Air Force Memorial Foundation Chairman H. Ross Perot, Jr., Secretary of Defense Donald Rumsfeld, Secretary of the Air Force Michael W. Wynne and Chief of Staff, United States Air Force General T. Michael Moseley respectively. The Air Force Memorial Foundation Board of Trustees, Chairman Major General Edward F. Grillo, Jr., USAF Retired and Vice President of Operations Colonel Peter W. Lindquist, USAF Retired were in attendance. Architect Kyle Johnson, representing the Pei firm, was present, and the Memorial's architect, James Ingo Freed, who had passed away in the last quarter of 2006, was poignantly missed.

Facing page:
Honor Guard sculpture,
weapon bearer
(at far left), detail

After the United States Air Force Band played a Prelude, the official ceremony began with the arrival of Donald Rumsfeld, Ross Perot, Jr., Michael W. Wynne, General T. Michael Moseley, and Chief Master Sergeant of the Air Force Rodney J. McKinley. President George W. Bush arrived later in the ceremony. The US Air Force Honor Guard made the Presentation of the Colors after which the United States Air Force Band accompanied the Singing Sergeants as they sang the National Anthem, and Master of Ceremonies, Bob Schieffer took the stage. Chaplain, Major General Donald J. Harlin, USAF, Retired, made the invocation.

Facing page:
Honor Guard sculpture,
flag bearer
(at middle left), detail

Following remarks by Mr. Perot and Chief Master Sergeant Rodney J. McKinley to a respectful audience, a video, *Spirit of the Air Force*, was shown.

A moving Aerial Review, *A Tribute to Airmen of Yesterday and Today*, was presented to a narrative written by Colonel Walter J. Boyne, USAF Retired. It was read while music written by the United States Air Force Band was performed. This tribute was arranged by Major General Grillo, Jr., USAF Retired. A fly-over of aircraft from the 1930s through current times included the B-17 and B-24 from World War II, B-2 Spirit and C-17 Globemaster III of the Global War on Terror, a four-ship "Heritage Flight," the F-86 Sabre, the F-4 Phantom, the F-15C Eagle and the F-22A Raptor.

The Higher We Fly, performed by The US Air Force Band and the Singing Sergeants followed Remarks by Chief of Staff of the Air Force General T. Michael Moseley and Secretary of the Air Force Michael W. Wynne.

Facing page:
Honor Guard sculpture, flag and battle streamer bearer (at middle right), detail

Remarks by Secretary of Defense Donald H. Rumsfeld were followed by those of President George W. Bush, before the Official Dedication of the Air Force Memorial. President Bush formally accepted the US Air Force Memorial on behalf of the Nation.

The finale of the Dedication was a breathtaking, heart pounding "Bomb Burst" maneuver performed by the United States Air Force's flight demonstration team, the Thunderbirds.

Facing page:
Honor Guard sculpture,
weapon bearer
(at far right), detail

Once molds are made, a select number of identical bronze sculptures may be cast from them. Traditionally, each additional cast combines with the first to be part of the same overall limited edition — each is considered an original work of art. Several additional casts of the Honor Guard sculpture created for Arlington National Cemetery were made from the molds with the permission of the Air Force Memorial Foundation.

On April 21, 2007, a second bronze cast of the Honor Guard sculpture for the United States Air Force Memorial in Arlington was dedicated at Randolph-Macon Academy, an Air Force Junior Reserve Officer Training Corps (AFJROTC) boarding school in Front Royal, Virginia. During official ceremonies marking the sculpture's dedication opposite historic Sonner-Payne Hall, Randolph-Macon Academy (R-MA) paid tribute to the proud traditions of the Air Force and Randolph-Macon's heritage in military service. The statue stands at R-MA through the generosity of the Academy's alumnus Harlan Crow of Dallas, Texas.

Randolph-Macon Academy was founded in 1892 and became an Air Force Junior ROTC unit in 1975. It was the first co-ed boarding school to do so, and it was the only co-ed boarding school with AFJROTC until the fall of 2005. Like many military schools, R-MA struggled during the 1970s and 1980s, coming dangerously close to closing its doors. The move to the AFJROTC program in 1975 is largely credited with saving the Academy, which today stands as one of the premier military boarding schools in the Nation.

Other installations of the Honor Guard sculpture include:
- Air Force Academy, Colorado Springs, Colorado
- Alliance Airport, Texas

Facing page:
Honor Guard sculpture
at Randolph-Macon
Academy, Front Royal,
Virginia, detail

About the Sculptor

The work of the sculptor Zenos Frudakis denotes more than mere self discipline, technical ability and the fundamental qualities of good sculpture. The sculptures exhibit a mobility, sensitivity and presence of the human figure that command the viewer's notice and respect. The sculptural forms are intensified when translated into bronze, which gives proof that such sculptures with beautiful forms and graceful presence can never be out-dated.

Duane Hanson
sculptor, 1991

Traditional Yet Contemporary

by William Innes Homer,
H. Rodney Sharp Professor
Emeritus, Department of Art
History, University of Delaware

Zenos Frudakis' sculpture deals with the urgent sense of reality in the human form. He reflects not the current fashions of modernism, but stylistic language grounded in thorough understanding of anatomy and construction. In the late nineteenth century, this knowledge, fostered by such schools as the Pennsylvania Academy of the Fine Arts, was considered the basis for good art. Now largely forgotten outside the realm of academies, and even at times within, this tradition has been weakened by the competing emphasis on expressionism and abstraction. But with Frudakis, a student at the Pennsylvania Academy between 1973 and 1976, realism is alive and well.

Looking at Frudakis' work, we feel the spirit of Thomas Eakins, teacher then director of schools of the Pennsylvania Academy (1876-1886). Eakins was principally a painter, but he was also a sculptor and he insisted that his students of painting develop a sense of form by modeling clay. For Eakins, too, anatomy and the grand construction of the figure were prime concerns. His students were expected to dissect cadavers of humans and animals, and he personally supervised many of these efforts. He insisted that his pupils ground their work in the real and visible, just as he did his own sculpture.

Thomas Eakins was expelled from the Academy in 1886, in the midst of a scandal precipitated by his all-too-frank exposure of the nude model to his classes. But Eakins' devotion to visual honesty and structural knowledge remained strong under his successor, Thomas Anshutz, a gifted teacher who served on the faculty until his death in 1913. Even in Anshutz' time, this earlier tradition flourished, and it has continued to characterize the Academy's distinctive methods of training to the present day, though with decreasing stress on anatomy. I recently visited the Academy's studios and glanced at a group of prize-winning student sculptures that had been retained over four or five decades. Except for the hair style, there was little difference in treatment of the model: a convincing command of the figure's structure and gesture was paramount.

When I first saw Frudakis' work, I immediately felt he belonged to the best of the Academy's traditions. His mature work of course, transcends the student sculptures just cited, for he became a master of gesture and movement. Although he does not profess to be a modernist, he has linked himself to certain contemporary ideas of lightness and fluidity of the form that would have been unknown in Eakins' time. And, of course, his interest in sculptural color places him in a realm different from Eakins, whose own works in plaster, wax and bronze did not elaborate the intrinsic hues of his materials. Frudakis' color is his concession to expressionism, though it elaborates on, rather than dominates, his fundamental conception of form.

Looking at Frudakis' work, we see something that is traditional, based on disciplined observation, yet definitely belonging to our time. In view of the current Postmodern nostalgia for the substantial values of the past, Frudakis' sculpture seems strikingly relevant today. His view is Postmodern, too, because of his professed social concerns. He could never step out of his own era, nor would he wish to.

Zenos Frudakis

Zenos' father, musician and poet Vasilis Frudakis, was born on Crete. His mother, Kassiani Alexis, was also Greek. She and her husband raised the Frudakis children with an awareness of Greek traditions, music and culture. Born in 1951 in San Francisco and raised in Wheeling, West Virginia, and then Gary, Indiana, Zenos admired Greek art, literature, and philosophy. The icons of Wheeling's Greek Orthodox Church both scared and fascinated Zenos as a small child. The stern faces of saints created to stimulate fear in the viewer, especially St. George, were among his earliest memories of portraiture.

Zenos created his first sculptures as a little child from dough given to him by his mother as she baked bread. In his first studio, under the kitchen table, he fashioned human figures out of bread dough.

The works of Rodin, Michelangelo, Bernini and Carpeaux inspired Zenos as well as poetry, especially that of Frost, Eliot, Roethke and Graves. Post-modern deconstructionalist philosophy shaped Zenos' thought and artistic style.

Initially, Zenos worked in the steel mills of Gary, Indiana. He came to Philadelphia in 1972 intent on studying at the Pennsylvania Academy of the Fine Arts. After seeing Zenos' drawings, Academy Dean Henry Hotz helped him obtain an unprecedented first-year scholarship from the Dolfinger-McMahon Foundation. Zenos then attended the University of Pennsylvania to obtain Bachelor and Master degrees in Fine Art. After college, he remained in the Philadelphia area to build his career.

Zenos earned commissions, honors and awards. Recommended by masters of American sculpture Walker Hancock and Donald DeLue for membership in the National Sculpture Society, voted in and quickly advanced to Fellow, Zenos won the Society's President's Prize, Gold Medal and numerous other awards in the juried annuals held in New York City. Voted into membership and advanced to Academician of the National Academy of Design, Zenos exhibited work in the National Academy's exhibitions. The only American invited to participate in Japan's Third Rodin Grand Prize Exhibition, he was awarded the Hakone Award at Utsukushi-ga-hara Open Air Museum in 1990. A cast of his sculpture Reaching, created through Indianapolis, Indiana's Percent for Art program, was purchased by the Museum.

A professional sculptor for over three decades, Zenos' works are placed locally, nationally and internationally.

For more information, please see www.zenosfrudakis.com.

Thoughts
on My Work
and the
Honor Guard
Commission

by Zenos Frudakis

My intent, in creating the Honor Guard sculpture, was to model statues of living figures. I sought to evoke distinct and diverse individuals with a beating heart beneath each uniform. Only then could I begin to achieve the imperative — that this contemporary sculpture embody such human qualities as honor and dignity.

The bronze figurative sculpture complements the large, abstract stainless spires. Together, they represent an essential aspect of the Air Force — the successful relationship of man and machine. The Honor Guard statue represents the men and women of the USAF. The spires symbolize their action in flight. Collectively they form a complete artistic statement. From a distance, the tall spires inspire, and draw the public in. The Honor Guard sculpture, presented on a human scale, reminds us that essentially, this Memorial honors individuals who have sacrificed to safeguard our freedoms. Both of these elements make the Memorial a special place for meditation and remembrance.

Recently at Arlington National Cemetery, as I stood next to the Honor Guard sculpture, I was startled by a not-so-distant boom. After a short pause, I heard it again. Before the third report, I realized what I was hearing, which a mournful bugle confirmed. Gradually, I had the terrible realization that this ceremony had been performed many times, and that it would be repeated often in the future. Standing at the Air Force Memorial, I could see the hillside of graves, knowing at that moment someone's passing was respectfully being marked with a 21-gun salute and taps. As I stood next to the bronze Honor Guard, I realized just how appropriate and meaningful it was for the figures to stand in attentive honor of those who have sacrificed their lives in the past as well as those who will follow in the future.

Facing page:
Honor Guard sculpture
with Memorial Wall

I feel honored to have been given the opportunity to create this sculpture.

Colophon

Editorial consultation and design
by Nathan Garland
in New Haven, Connecticut.

Set in a contemporary version
of a classic typeface cut by Nicholas Kis,
often called Janson.

This first edition of five thousand books
was printed on archival paper
in four-color process and duotone in Italy
by Amilcare Pizzi.

All photographs are by Zenos Frudakis
except pages 49 and 52–53,
which are by Callie Bangyekan.